Daydreams and Shadows

Written by Ani Rumaer

PublishAmerica
Baltimore

ISBN: 1-60610-668-6
PUBLISHED BY PUBLISHAMERICA, LLLP
www.publishamerica.com
Baltimore

Printed in the United States of America

Dedication

To my dear friends and family who have endured with me though indirectly in the sacrifice to which I made in completing this book, and who with deep love and patience have allowed me to be as I am— eccentric and free; I say with a most sincere heart, thank you.

Ani Rumaer

To Steffon

Ani Rumaer

Our hearts will always be connected—

your friend.

April 1, 2009

Special thanks to William Cook.
Your eyes saw more than mine.

Table of Contents

Invocation

Reader—there is something to be said here at the very beginning which, I believe, is of importance to you.

I have discovered that one of our most important duties in this life is that we ought to live it with a deep sense of dignity and courage: the first helps us to rise above the ordinary; the second helps us to live extraordinary lives.

And wherever God has placed each one of us in life, it is there—in that particular time and place—that we ought to put our best efforts towards fulfilling whatever special calling that has been inspired within us. This we ought to do right where we stand.

In seeking to meet that goal, we then honor both God and ourselves. The experience of living, of being human, is one that none of us can shirk: this is our most important business and duty, one which we ought to satisfy as best as we can so that we might become magnanimous and happy in life. This is the true and ultimate destiny of every human being.

A. R.
Love, Faith and Destiny

To My Reader

What my natural inspiration drew out of me is all that is contained in this book, and my intent on publishing it was only to share with you. If by chance, however, the contents of this book happen to mirror some semblance of the manifold interests that life holds for you, for me, and for everyone else then, perhaps, the reader might agree that there is some worth here. So let me begin by saying what spurred me on to write.

Of my many tender feelings that I had been experiencing in the course of my life, like scattered seeds, they remained buried yet tilling within. This sowing, however, eventually had its bloom in the fields of poetry. From my heart, I have brought out into the world what is intimate and true to me, which now rest in these poems of mine. The work itself is a product of both imagination and reality, but it is hard to say where one begins and the other ends, yet the themes which they depict do touch upon feelings that are universal to all of us.

I did early on in my life experience an awakening. The exact time that it happened, I do not remember; that episode, however, was a turning point in my life: an experience which was more a sign of what I may now refer to a personal calling.

To search, to learn, and to uncover more of what is true in me and in the world is a need that daily goads me. This yearning is the spring of my enthusiasm: a feeling that directs me toward a kind of private work, so to speak. I did feel this need from the very beginning, but time had not yet made it my season for such work for I was in need of both substance and growth. What I had lacked in knowledge and in growth, I did, however, acquire from long hours of meditative reading and many more spent in putting pen to paper, a practice which is still the main spring of much of my work.

There were certain powerful feelings that had guided me to where I now stand. They have demanded, in a kind of way, their own existence and expression. Thus, they have enabled me, if I may say so, to feel the world.

The truth of the matter is that we are all capable of feeling, of sensing, of involving ourselves in the world. Because of this, we are by a kind of natural attraction drawn within the manifolds of reality: in one sense—we are caught within its net, in another—we are not so entangled that we lack the freedom to exist therein. By simply living, we stream through our daily experience just like current through a wire; we interpret what life is in this way. The senses plug us in and convey feelings which allow us to become both a participant and a spectator of reality. The mind, too, can even transform all that we feel. It can send us back to the past or it can carry us forward to what is yet to come. Why, then, is this important? Let me tell you.

Like a fish in water, life surrounds us; it is all about us even inside of us. We all share in a common experience of that immersion; we share in all of the many elements that compose life itself.

We have all, for example, been touched by feelings of love and anger, pain and pleasure, gain and loss, sorrow and—of course—happiness, some of us more, others less. Such feelings are, indeed, the sinews that link us universally; they weave us into the tapestry of life—for better or for worse. On this last point, we may all seem agreed, especially on the effects that those feelings can have upon our hearts. Thus, what I now present in this book reflects shades of those universal elements that all of us, in the course of our lives, are bound to be touched by.

Born from what were my loves, loses, sorrows, and happiness, a myriad of feelings emerged within only to sink deeper than before; yet it was from that ocean of feelings that I distilled these poems. From when I first began this book, my hope was like rivulets that run toward a grand river filling it with their richness that this book would fill you; that its contents would settle towards the grandest river of them all—the one flowing within.

So I allow you to enter through those doors that lead to me. The part of who I am that I have been most patiently at work to set free, so that I might unfasten the many ties that hold it within the imperceptible walls that tower from way down in the depths of my being. Scattered here, then, in this book are those memories of Daydreams and Shadows.

Prologue

I have ever to find a sea shell that I have patience for.

From My Journal
Early morning note

No sun ever sets in the mind's eye.

F.M.J.
Evening note

Loves reap but little return when they sow themselves in shallow soil.

F.M.J.
Midnight note

A River Runs

A River runs deep
that murmurs quieter than the Mississippi sleeps.

A River runs deep
that carries sediments of clay-made souls that fall and meet.

A River runs deep
that travels straight through holy sanctums that hallow beneath.

A River runs deep
where eternal banks shoulder the flow towards that sacred delta.

A River runs deep
spilling its spirit into an ocean of dreams.

A River runs deep
that flows rhythmically like an eternal heart beat.

A River runs deep…

Always Beyond

Always beyond we seem to be
existing out there, somewhere, ever
falling into the past yet stepping into the future.

Rarely are we home
to answer the calls of the present.

What then truly belongs to us?

That is why we miss felicity so much
because we are rarely here and always elsewhere.

What a pity that we look so far for what is so near.

No loss of memory really ruins us
because we always seem to pay forward
for what has yet to come—like insurance—and
we owe on credit what we have used already.

And though the stars beam all about
they too will eventually dim and blow out.

Be an architect then and design the present:
make it beautiful, for this is our true home.

Awakening

Having nearly lost the breath of everyday experience,
now I daily birth new passions for it.

I am consumed by it; the passion insinuates every
mortal cell of my being.

Drawn from an inkwell of colorful desires,
a portrait slave I have been painted.

Experience—moment by moment—
precipitates me with eager lessons
whose aim is ever straight, never crooked.

Of my dreams,
well, they restlessly walk within my temple walls
depositing things that crowd my heart—a room
that time had so long ago shut.

Yet with rugged strength,
I tunnel toward that sacred under-world
digging up things and
piling them into life's cache like treasure stones:
those remembrances—those
artifacts of a flung past,
which daily I carry back into the most sacred of places.

The eyes even now grow ripe with curiosity
though the heart remains spoiled by fugitive passions.

Time indeed tells us no tales that never are we above loss.

Bed of Roses

Oh, gentle world I beseech an open ear
for life ain't no bed of roses anywhere.

Serene is the rose that parades its bright petals
though bitter are its thorns that remain still and settled.

All above seems as happy as can be,
yet just below waits unseen misery.

Life, for sure, ain't no bed of roses anywhere!

Things can never be happy every waking hour
both high and low will taste some sweet, some sour,
though never at the exact same hour.

So, my friend, remember.

Life ain't no bed of rose anywhere.

Beloved

You be still my heart
like eyes that gaze at the moon,

and like eager waves that crash into the shore
my love for you has turned from a pulse to a boom.

Your touch has weathered my coarse soul
and your love has textured my life.

My heart grows with fever when I think of you,
yet the only remedy is your love,
for no other will do.

You be still my heart
with your divine magic…indeed.

That when near you my heart turns electric,
but when you're far it surges.

Sleep carries me away when the day bends and falls,
and patience guards me all the while until the night surrenders to me once
more.

And always before I wake,
fresh memories of you rise with me to greet the dawning new day.

Birthday

The Days come and go like a train of time,

and like the rising sun the future will shine.

Loses—these get forgotten with every passing moment
though real possessions time never takes away.

So wait patiently, if you can,
the coming joys move slowly but are never delayed.

Listen to the soul, for it quietly speaks.

And the heart—only true love can unlock it,
and happiness—it too will come though little by little.

Yes, the Days, indeed, come and go,
and like the love of sun and sea each new one will kiss your memory.

But of all the days that come, your Birthday is truly a special one.

So bask in it as if it were your special sun.

Bounded

Pulled we are by many strings in this life.

Like rainfall, we are bound to be touched
in one way or another by whatever comes our way.

That our sorrows may echo loudly across the heartland
giving strength to old memories
of what experience has taught us.

The end, hold back as long as you can,
and then kiss time good bye courageously.

For a long tale we could tell though a life is measured short.

That we leave promises unfulfilled
that had no real measure when we made them;
therefore let time write them off and start anew.

To leave soon before we have given life its just due
is but a half-life.

Better are we for leaving behind no small regrets
because we lose more when we forget
to love, to desire, and to promise.

For when the lamp dims like a fading sun,

we will burn away old desires,
old dreams, old loves too;
then we will surrender them to a place more homely than this one.

What is better than to see the setting of the sun peacefully?

That to know the hand that created all
will embrace us once more,
and that memory is but a single flash of that eternal light;
for time will hold us true
to some promises, to some desires, to some dreams.

So treasure the heart and all its real possessions,
for true happiness is buried there deep
within that sacred place.

Coming and Going

Though I know that I will fade into memory
to be lost as an erasure in temporal minds,

I do hope to leave something of a remnant behind,
if only a shade of what was to be,
so that time may not fully shut the eternal doors to my memory.

Every beginning leads to an end;
I daily refresh the mind of this.

And toward that heavenly toll I daily turn myself
to listen for the silence that frees everything within.

Days and Dreams and Shadows

In the eternal ocean of memory,
my Days and Dreams and Shadows
have dissolved themselves completely,

and there they rise and fall and fade
into the vastness of eternity.

But before, in the land of appearances,
they had been no more than passing illusions.

That upon the walls of the soul my Shadows were
painted, my Dreams too had spun themselves
into web-like tapestries to keep me whole,
and each Day kissed my eyes with a growing
verdure of fresh curiosities.

Now there in memory's ocean these Days and Dreams and Shadows
still swim.

Destiny Calls

Destiny calls to me from that deep
sleep of illusion.
I hear it faintly though pretense deafens me some.

The voice of the Shadow bellows low and
the still night brings with it more than sleep, lessons.

And when I wake some time later
the Shadow is no more,
yet left behind are remnants of ghostly
memories that flicker in and out of the mind's eye
showing me what possibilities
still lay buried in this mortal statue.

Plentiful, indeed, are the treasures of the heart though
few truly know them,
for this is why to dream, to find her—Destiny.

Go and wonder…
Love life—then the Shadow will come.
What a charming guide to have…

So dare to dream
then the heart will become a lamplight for your happiness.

Dreams

Of dreams,
none will ever see a single sunset,
for they paint themselves upon an
eternal rainbow of memory.

Yet dreamers seem to always end;
they lose of days and nights in the fall.

And the loom of creation hails all of that,
then time makes all things pray
tallying their hours and their deeds,
payment always in full, no credit.

For sure the old stage withers,
for everything has its season,
never spirit though.

To have been once a prop, now an altar;
to have gazed, now to sleep—
in the end, all turns to scenery.

Dreams, too, weather then erode
turning themselves into little things
to be scattered across the immortal canvas of time.

Eternal Mind

Time may be a pirate of what we possess,
but never of our imagination—this is eternally free.

That we frame the world through apprenticed eyes,
yet we paint it with a beautiful mind.

Yes…
Time may be a pirate of what we possess,
but never of our imagination—this is eternally free.

Equality

Equality disunites, never frees,
and though we rise to equal measure across the whole
we stand feeble, still, and alone.

We are set free by our natural spirit,
yet hemmed in by the public will.

All do seem to breathe the air of the mass
though their opinions go unexamined once they have passed.

Some do dare to march without the majority's consent,
but the mass weighs so heavily on such dissent.

When all that we hear is the public voice
who truly makes an independent choice.

Equality disunites, link—by—link.
And so we lose touch of the self in an unstable dream.

How, then, can the free be free when led by anxious minds?

We see daily how rewards get passed from hand to hand,
for this is how equality elevates all to a parallel stand.

The mass indeed runs us straight each and every day,
for it carries us hesitantly without delay.

And though we join in this specialized race
we find that in time the majority is still behind pace.

Yes, equality—truly—dis—unites.

Exhumed

Of all my memories,
yours I daily call from their depths
and each time I do they drown me into
an ocean of dreams.

There they eclipse my self-made world
showing me the now and the then,
the real and the make-believe.

Then an under-current of memories
carries me down
into a torrent of emotions
causing me to lose my senses,

yet I rise to the surface
only to feel the pull of them once more.

And then like a sun among suns,
these memories of you radiate my senses anew
filling them with full satisfaction.

And as night wakes to play in the moon's madness,
I fall under a spell of missing you,

and again, I go in search of you,
and once more I find you there—a diamond, buried in my imagination.

Faith

Giving way to the love of gravity they leapt;
their bodies plummeted head-long toward a bed of fate
taking with them mortality to its final destination.

Then the wind gave a sigh of relief,
"Surrender is never easy," she whispered,
"though it frees reality from illusion."

All dreams eventually break then the dreamer wakes—how true!

Nothing more comes after the fall was the story told them;
this belief was glued to their hearts more than ever before.

And with a sudden swooping catch,
the angels save them
and restored the light of hope in them
then lifted them beyond the earth and sky.

Felicity

Of whatever future felicity that we wish,
it is the mirror life that reveals our true happiness.

And of all our days that see the sun,
we must see them joined but never done.

Of whatever power we may naturally possess,
it is only courage that guards our tender happiness.

And of all the things we gain along the way,
we stand to risk their loss each and every day.

So whatever blessings we get from fortune's hands,
we keep them safe by making noble plans.

Then always a friend should wisdom be,
for it is the best guide for living happily.

Fever

You are ever the wind that lifts
me beyond the clouds.

Your flow runs straight through me
like currents of ecstasy.

A snake charmer you are
moving me
this way and that way,
sway to sway—
slowly, sensually, wildly.

And your sweet scent
is candy for my soul,
the sugar to all my dreams.

And though morn compels me
to wake and surrender you,

it is the night, however, that calls me
back to memory's altar to pray
you mine again.

You're my Turkish moon
stirring me mad with dreams of you,

and through it all we wander
in the fever of love

from dusk—till—dawn.

Flung Stone

What ever great little things
we hope to be
this is ours to endure.

And through the channels of time
the years, the days, the countless moments
span across that eternal medium
that we must swim to reach our possibilities.

That the sleepless hero
may, at any moment,
break through
and enter the world;
then, perhaps,
courage will take wing and lift us
to that extraordinary plane.

That to pray to ourselves divine yet temporal,
and to incline ourselves against God's grace
is a sure gain, always.

Never shall we rise above those eternal limits
so that we learn to trust
that something more is to come
from all that we do here.

For we are bounded by the necessity
of Him that pervades and insinuates all things.

And that we ought to never give hymn,
nor praise,
to no wanderer deity
that pretends to grant entrance to things made
through the gates of eternity.

That to grasp at such a hard and heavy lie
is but a flung stone, one which is often
throne by the devil himself.

Forest

A rose garden sits alone in a patch of Earth
in a remote part of the Forest
waiting for the rain to come.

Worms dig in and out
leaving the rest of the partly cleansed Earth
for the rain to fully purify.

Branches patiently
sway giving cool breeze
to birds nestled in the bark.

Ants scurry along busily
managing order and business as usual.

II

The rain must be delayed,
or stuck in the clouds,
or maybe filling up its tank.

The bugs are climbing all over slimy
rocks to gather their food;
thousands or maybe even millions
forage over this partly cleansed Earth.
Oh, look, here comes a parade of sable clouds.

The roses seem to know that the rain is coming
with their petals sprung wide open.
And ants must smell the freshness in the air
because they have started their orderly march home.

III

Look! The bugs seem stirring with confusion.
I wonder why?
Yes, they too know that rain
can carry them far and away.

Indeed, it really looks like the rain is coming.

I guess the tension
in the Forest will be relieved soon
and the ground will finally
get its face muddied up again.

IV

Almost everything seems still but the rain.
It sounds so good in the Forest.

I will let the Forest play with the rain
and say goodbye to the rose garden that sits alone
in a patch of Earth
in that remote part of the Forest.

The rain is falling hard now,
and the partly cleansed Earth will soon be purified.

Heart Wake

Of love's fading sun
the eyes empty shut.

The heart's satisfactions always stir with
our present sorrows: a mix of the bitter and sweet.

To be pitied is the heart that had no time
to treasure old affinities.

So keep the eyes narrow and serene,
and plant them far from superfluity,
for felicity is always found in the little things.

Hold Fast to Dreams

Hold fast to dreams,
for like new born birds
they dare to fly.

Hold fast to dreams,
for sure, some will fall like
the evening tide.

Hold fast to dreams,
for new ones will always rise high.

Hold fast to dreams,
for when all about seems to fade,
they like wine, can grow and refine with age.

Hold fast to dreams,
for they can sail you across vast seas
to land you upon shores of new discoveries.

Hold fast…to dreams…

Hope's Place

Hope has a place
where hearts can weep
and tired souls sleep.

Hope has a place
where storms never rage
and fields are always serene.

Hope has a place
where dreams come true
and desires are but few.

Hope has a place
where imagination is free
and soul remains new.

Hope has a place
where skies are always blue
and rivers run through and through.

Hope has a place…

I Will

Stand anywhere
I will
to greet Destiny.

Go anywhere
I will
to fulfill the Dream.

Wait anytime
I will
to meet Love.

Befriend anyone
I will
to know Trust.

Give anything good
I will
to show Goodness.

Let any loss go
I will
to Mature.

Set any sorrow free
I will
to feel Happiness.

And through it all,
remain hopeful
I will
to see the End.

Journey

Ever will the spell of time break
to set free all destinies

then it will open them up
to new and bountiful fields of discovery
so that they may have of days
what nature has bequeathed upon all souls:
to dream, to desire, to love, and hope.

These are both map and compass
showing all their way through life.

Land of Mine

Color me that country that braves the Atlantic sea;

color me that country that wrestles the westward breeze;

color me that country where rainbows dye the earth so beautifully.

II

Color me that country where eagles soar through vanilla skies;

color me that country where the coastal sea ushers in crimson tides;

color me that country of teeming hopes and milling dreams;

color me that country where crumbs feed the displeased.

III

Color me that country of infamous glory across troubled seas;

color me that country of strange fruit trampled by sovereign feet;

color me that country where pillars rise and paint the night sky;

color me that country where work is pride and patriots live to die.

IV

Color me that country of half-born dreams that flow merrily down streams;

color me that country where mothers' sons fall at dawn for distant dreams;

color me that country where Liberty sleeps from dusk till morn;

color me that country of soulful songs and jazzy beats;

color me that country where sleep never sleeps.

V

Color me that country where eyes look discreet when they peek;

color me that country of private charms that seduce the meek;

color me that country where backs shun the pride of the land;

color me that country of trick and trade and gay parades;

color me that country of unschooled Moments and half-lit stars.

VI

Color me that country where the crowds walk with uneasy feet;

color me that country of foreign hopes and domestic conceit;

color me that country of supermen and wonder women;

color me that country of half-made souls and full-bred illusions;

color me that country where the morning pulse stirs everywhere.

VII

Color me that country where a name is holy;

color me that country where honor has a face of green;

color me that simple but beautiful color:

color me in that red, in that white, in that blue.

Color me America.

Legend

Bold was the vision of a panacea
since the early dawn,
one that endeavors to always light the darkness.

But time may carry us far into the future
and leave us there
exiled at the outpost of progress.

For if we dim the lamplight within,
the darkness, for sure, will come.

Yet it is there in the pitch black
that our courage can shine
and turn us into Legends:

to look back for guidance,
to look within for courage,
and to dream ahead of what might be.

Letters Between Us

The letters, their content,
and why they came to be—all of that
even with my best hopes
could not have held back the concatenation
of events that inevitably led to my love's demise.

There were letters between us.
I did write to them: first one, then a second.

For I had imagined her parents
were somewhat more,
for the simple reason that she, their daughter,
was more in my eyes.

But I had naively given to them
a measure of respect that one often gives to those
close to the one we are in love with at the time.

To tell them of what I had discovered
about her, their daughter,
and why my heart had become swollen with love
for her was why I had written the first.

And how all of that had fallen to ruins was
the reason for the second.

II

At the beginning,
my heart was anxious and eagerly desirous;
but like a dam,
I held so much back:
I restrained the pounding pressure of my heart,
and what I could not contain there,
I siphoned off to the upper channels of my mind.

I had turned my heart's valves nearly shut through
it all.
For I had learned later on that when we venture
into the fields of love,
we will always encounter thorns and pricks and
blades of sharp grasses.

III

Rarity is often a treasure in life,
this I did think of her;
this I did write in the first letter.

Then time had spun its web
weaving so many unforeseen
events, which no doubt
brought about the end.

For she had lit my mind as fulgent as the sun,
and with hands like da Vinci's,
she had painted upon my soul,
for she had loved me many miles deep;
all that she had wanted was me.

Because of them, however, the keepers of both
her mind and, as it seemed to me, her soul,
this pregnancy of love ended still born;
for they had blindly judged it, denounced it, and
ultimately condemned the affair.

From that sprang a conspiracy of plots and plans
which became a war upon my reason but a peace for their ignorance

For their happiness, she had sabotaged hers.
How noble yet ruinous, I thought to myself.

Yes, letters were sent,
but my instincts assured me
that their contents never met their eyes.

I did imagine though that they now laid somewhere
among a mass of refuse in some far away place
for only the wind to gape at.

IV

Denial always seems to be the right path to detour the truth:
this they did indeed.

We are never fixed to any one world when it comes to love.
Yes, she and I were from other worlds, so it seemed in the end.
But things will always fall apart when courage is absent from the heart; what
love can do for the heart ignorance can never do for the mind.

In estimating the love of her by them,
I intimated that their affection was a seething animosity
darting from their private hearts though its aim was me.

Heavy with anxiety, a fragile mind will always hem happiness in,
not only its own, but others.

So this love affair went like the wind,
one that was yet to bloom,
one that left two hearts rift of syncopation.

Liberty

Liberty,
the world calls you from your deep sleep,
for you slumber too long in quiet memory.

Liberty,
ship your dreams across life's vast sea,
for many are born with no peace then die never free.

Liberty,
though I petition thee, sleep you still keep;
yet so many dare to sail alone across those troubled waters
beating their oars of freedom churning white the sea.

Oh, Liberty, hear me!
Set sail across freedom's ocean so that many may see the sun free.

Liberty,
the bell tolls loudly to end your untroubled dreams.

Wake, friend! Wake!

There is much time you keep,
that much is owed to the cries of the meek.

The world still calls, friend.
Hear them! Hear them now!

Give them grand justice, nothing less, nothing cheap.

Get up and go—everywhere—and deliver yourself
as a gift of peace
and forever brake the shackles of cowardly sleep.

Life Ain't No Permanent Press

Life has to be ironed out.

We have to smoothen out the wrinkles,
press out the ends,
unravel the creases that lie underneath.

We have to add some heat to it,
for things will always get rumpled up.

So press it out—everyday,
press a little here, press a little there,
always looking more carefully each time
for the wrinkles that the eyes missed,
especially the ones that make life look unkempt.

Yes, life ain't no permanent press;
it has to be ironed out.

We have to continue to press it
even though we ironed it yesterday.

For only we can make it look decent and beautiful.

So press on…
add some heat to it…
and the wrinkles will melt away,
the ends will straighten out,
the lengths will to.

In the end,
life will look good,
it will be decent and free from being unkempt.

Life Jacket

A life is but a ripple in the ocean of reality,
and all of us are ever battered by the crash of
the wind heaving waves of our daily experience.

But faith and courage will always
buoy us up through the storms.

Love Joy

Of what the day may bring,
it is your beauty that shines upon my memory;

for it is your heart that mine beats for,
it is your love that gives me pleasure.

You and I have become woven together like night
and day out of the loom of desire and happiness,

and so shall we be now and eternally.

Love Mismeasured

For a very long time a clouded past
which had been stirring within
suddenly turned a mirror of cold reality.

In a flash,
all of what I had left behind
since that time of foreign love was now
rising from that dark abyss.

II

The train had not yet arrived at the station
though sounds of its approach I did hear faintly.

The platform stood as a dock of barrenness
with only me as its host,
yet it seemed teeming with a crowded silence,
the kind that one awakens to in reflection.

The distance walked since I entered the station
was a short one,
and near the edge I was now standing.

III

But it was there near the edge that my eyes glued themselves
to only sign hanging above the track.

"A restive heart always goes beyond its license,"
were the only words printed on it.

I read them, then a second, but it was the
third that had churned the whole of my being.

I had pulled my eyes away quick yet shyly
and tossed them straight towards the end
of the platform near the mouth of tunnel where the light from the
on-coming train began to dimly peer through.

IV

The words and their meaning had
dissolved themselves into me
like acid through raw matter.

The whole of my existence, for that moment,
seemed as if it began and ended right there,
in the station, on that platform.

Cold was the feelings I felt inside,
which caused me to no longer walk but trot
toward the ventilation at the end, which seemed strong and rejuvenating.

Every single part of me seemed strange to the rest;
the legs trembled, the hands swung senselessly,
the eyes blinked wildly,
and the face—it felt like a mass of sculpted pain.
All of me felt pregnant with an unexplainable anxiety.

V

But moments later the mind did reveal to me why.
I was a fool because I had love beyond reservation—beyond
love's proper measure.

Having reached the end,
the one light from the train turned two,
and the train swooshed out from the tunnel
with a furious rush.

I was bathed in the gushing air
which evaporated the drizzle of sweat
that had rained upon my face.

Then with a glance upward at the sign,
I did concede as to why I had suffered so;
for I had love with only my senses, not my reason;
for I had allowed the light within to grow dim and flicker out, with her.

VI

The train by then had stopped, the doors had opened,
and I gave a final but quick survey of the station;
it was still empty like me.

but as I stepped onto the train, at that very moment,
the hollowness which had then filled me
was being displaced with a calm feeling of acceptance;
for I had made a regrettable mistake,
one which we ought never to make:
to love another beyond oneself.

Love Stone

Daily I set myself aflame in the heart,
yet nightfall dims me little by little
leaving behind embers to light my renewal.

Love's wholeness never keeps long.

So I draw my lips to that eternal spring
so that I may drink of your memories
to quench my parched soul.

Never is time late but early is it to leave all lovers;
for only special memories can nurse a sick heart.

So each time I wake,
I lose a bit of you,
and like a fugitive mind
I run wildly missing you.

Yet time does come around again
only to find me near empty
then it fills me brimful with memories of you.

And like a stone's love for gravity,
I feel the same for you.

Time soon enough pulls me to the surface;
the sun breaks, and the dream scatters
like puffs of smoke.

Love's Arrows

Flung by hand
love's arrows go—an
aim charged to stake the heart's noble cargo.

Then to lay hands
upon clay-made sons,
a rosy color all hearts will run.

Of what was born under
a fall morning sun,
the spring makes new loves
when the old one is done.

For this is the way that all
of love's arrows go—an
aim charged to stake the heart's noble cargo.

Love's Deferment

Her fading words left
footprints on my memory,
and shortly thereafter
I followed them,
they led me to a silent place,
one of depth and breadth.

And while there
a discovery I made—their true meaning
and why she said them.

In a moment's pause,
a newly born wisdom rose up within me;
I did surrender to it, and with that acceptance
I felt assured that all would be well with me.

II

Then on my way back from that place,
yet another discovery I made,
one that only time could help us to find.

For my heart was hungry for love then:
I was eager to eat of its pleasures and
to gorge of its healing powers.

For with her,
all my hopes were made real,
and what was now gone, what I had lost,
was by no means a play of chance.

III

Until they leave us, loves never feel real enough
that our true feelings we naturally defer for an appointed time.

With this revelation, the spell of sorrow broke
refracting all through me like beams of sunlight.

Once more I had felt the full strength of memory
that both my past pain and happiness were seeds of necessity,
events of both circumstance and consequence.

And, now, the appointed time had come
for me to end my love's deferment;
to set free love's rejuvenating power.

And with this solitary thought,
I yielded willingly to the many new
hopes that now laid germinating in a future yet born,
one that held possibilities of new loves and happiness.

Love's Ocean

If love's ocean were to turn
a desert under me then
my hopes would rain upon it
and turn it full again;
I would sail my heartship across it to find you.

I would cast desire's sail high
to drape myself from the sun's eye;
I would travel by day and by night
never fearing the storm, nor its roar,
but only to hold fast as any true love would
showing no sign of surrender.

But if failure were to seize me,
know that I will go down
with the ship, never surrendering.

This would be my greatest victory
because I dared to love you.

So keep your arms open,
set flame to your heart,
for then I will see your sign
and know that you love me.

And when I land upon your shore
that flame of yours shall lead me to you.

So until then,
wait for me—patiently—if you can,

but lose no measure of love for me,
surrender not one ounce of faith in me,
and know that I love you like sea loves the sun,
and, in time, our hearts will beat as one.

Me

Touch me like the morning air.
Warm me like the evening sun.
Chill my fiery heart like a snowy day.

Be still my eyes like a rose in bloom.
Free my love like wishes of the heart.
Move me like the ocean's waves.

Never leave me like a birth mark.
Always watch me with curious eyes.
Kiss me like a first kiss.
And love me as the last day.

Read me like a good book.
Hide me as an old secret.
Call me like a missed friend.
Forgive me like a careless pet.

See me as a paradise found.
Think me as a new joy that never ends.
Bury me like treasures of the heart.
And Remember me as a never ending story.

Pale Love

Is a Pale love
like leaves that were never green
that neither sees
the spring nor summer months,
then to be swept away by the
fall breeze?

Or does it make us pray
like waking flowers
that summon the early
morning sun?

Can a Pale love ever quench the
heart's eternal thirst
which makes us wait like
a patient desert for the rain
to come?

How, then, can a Pale love
ever grow full of color
if it is shrouded and absent from
the light?

For sure,
such a love is a dry leaf
that falls, crumples and dies
then it vanishes with a gust of wind
that blows by.

Past and Remembrance

I did not imagine she had loved me
but she was the cause of its bloom.

The walk, the open field, the fading day—
all of this caused to settle in me a swelling sense of loss
that suddenly burst to empty despair.

And with a long glance backward from where I had crossed over—
standing there on the pale, green grass
the beat of my heart turned from a patter to a wild boom.

A trance of remembrance had gripped me
and a dead weight my heart had become,
and that stretch of pain which held it—grew strong
pulling me down to my knees.

The ground had become both my prop and altar,
and that patch of earth seemed holy now;
it was there that pain eulogized me,
and cowering and trembling sorrow began to fill me brimful.

It was then that the fever of lost love rose to its zenith.

For it was her that I had loved
so vividly, so passionately, so brightly,
and because I did, looming over me now was dark uncertainty.

II

Tears began to drizzle from my eyes
committing themselves to the parched grass below.
In seeing this, the mind then lifted them up
from their settled graves more alive than ever before;
those captured moments of her.
Every single one touched me
taking from me the very warmth of my soul—
degree by degree.

I had turned a cocoon of self-made sorrow,
all within had undergone a sort of metamorphosis of pain
and a kind of refraction of remembrance.

Even my words struggling to free themselves
had suffocated senselessly and painfully
for bitter reality had already shut their only escape.

III

I was broken because it was her I loved
as the earth loves the rain.

Still something else I did lose;
a passionate light she had taken from me.

So I rummaged the mind for those scattered rudiments of hope
believing I might by confession be healed
and by requital be redeemed;
but this I knew could never be.

I had yielded little to this fever of pain
and with remorseless hands

I gripped it, I tore at it, I wrenched at my chest
to rip away the pain,
and in doing so some was emancipated.

But like a flock of birds,
my memories crowded behind each other, one—by—one,
taking peel of me without pity.

God gave me sense
but it was she who took it away;
the passion which was once my own,
now gone, my heart regretfully yearned for.

IV

It seemed that all my hopes had turned criminal,
for her public denial was her betrayal and my secret disgrace;
this was her crime and my punishment.

Then those remembrances of things past
had now taken their last peel of me,
and that cold shame
which had covered me moments before
had turned a blanket of renewal.

Only foolish hearts leave their private felicity to go elsewhere,
whispered the last memory.

Then the parade of drifting clouds
that had hung high in the sky now had opened themselves up to me,
and those fleeting rays peering through
began to evaporate my fallen tears.

V

I had indeed before pleased my mind and my heart
perhaps all too well.
Not only the part of reason
but also the part of desire.

And while I was with her
my reason had too narrow a limit to roam;
my desires too wide a field to wander:
these could never be married faithfully.

And like scattering dust, the trance did eventually dissipate.
My tears, my pain, and those resurrected memories all went just the same.

In knowing what had been lost
and what was to be most desired,
I rose from that earthy altar
realizing that hidden love is never worth
its equal measure of pain;
for never could secrecy make bloom
what can only blossom in the light.

Questions

How many hearts have I slowed to a pulse?
How many roses have I stopped short of bloom?
How many desires have I tamed?
How many kindnesses have I brushed away?
How many loves have I caused to fade?
How many rivers of tears have I caused to flow?
How many lies have been of my prop and altar?
How many illusions have I made my reality?
How many hopes have I lost to memory?
How many times have I feared to dare?
How many hearts have I inspired?
How many pleasures have I enjoyed?
How many lessons have I learned?
How long have I denied destiny?
How many…

Risk

All is risk but the end.

We grip the rope of chance
to climb on up the totem pole of uncertainty;

for long is the hope of all possibilities
and short is its guarantee.

Yet we risk and play with potentialities
day in—and—day out.

We romp with life to seek some good
though nothing gives fullness to such a pledge.

Yet we hold on to hope so that we may keep from
slipping over the edge of infinity.

It is better to be brave
to set ourselves a noble challenge.

And whether we advance a victor or
retreat a defeater,
the worth, the risk,
can never be judged before, only after.

Somnia

Though the dream did end;
all the while it had been nothing more than an illusion,
one that time had not yet freed.

But when he discovered
love, faith, and destiny,
the illusion shattered
then the reverie freed him.

Sorrow's Path

God spared me and
carried me to that place where sorrow roams.

Why?
To show me the heart's way, the pathway of hope—
a trail that time never departs,
the only road to felicity.

And along that way,
shards of life's crystal ball are scattered about never to be put back again;

for all memories are individuals,
they stand alone and are never the same.

God indeed spares us from a long tuition
when we yield to sorrow and follow its path.

Sovereign Wings

The flight had seemed dependent upon borrowed wings.

This belief had kindled inside for a long while,
yet it was pretense that showed me the way.

Alone, above in a patch of sky, hovering
the eyes saw a plume of clouds—
full of puff and curve—
pulling and pushing of their own free will.

All begins with a nudge,
but after that,
all is gravity,
all is attraction,
all is about the flow.

Revelation always frees disbelief showing both its cause and effect.

For the eyes did reveal this to me,
that all the while sovereign wings lifted me;

thereafter, I soared even higher than before.

Specter

The Specter of the times lives well,
and life's market daily buys and sells.

In the burning sands, flowers bloom,
and in conquerors' lands rear foes anew.

All seemingly stirs to and fro,

and School masters give birth to their servants;
the Moments make their anthems beam across channels.

Vast marvels tempestuously seduce those motley senses
while the moon rises and the sun falls.

Goading appetites hunt them daily though their bellies churn full.

Fugitive desires trouble their sleep's charm;
hunger eagerly rouses their felicity,
and their souls animate hollowly.

Spirits suffuse them and they muddle their gait through the night,
and their buildings bury their hearts' tender plans.

The promise land looms over the horizon,
but none have sovereign bonds,
yet all remain island-safe.

The Storm

The storm came and touched their hearts
breaking them with its thunder clap;
their hearts fell and shattered
then the world in one moment
turned a turbulent sea.

Yet they kept themselves for the coming
light that comes after all passing storms.

Meanwhile, patience guarded their tender hearts;
courage shielded them against sorrow's arrows,
and their hopes turned a canopy against the bitter darkness.

Then sun came mending each piece that had fallen
with the power that stirs wingless birds to dream.

And with tender eyes they look beyond
and saw that love is real, faith is real, destiny is real.

Then time freed them and unlocked
their gated happiness.

The storm began to dissipate,
its thunder fell silent,
and the wind's howl grew to a sleeping murmur
putting all that had happened to rest again.
The light of day shone and the storm was no more.

To Be

Before my eyes close,
I hope to see…

Before my last breath goes,
I hope to say…

Before my ears go silent,
I hope to hear…

Before my heart beats no more,
I hope to be…

And if none of these come to pass
then
I hope to dream…

The Trust

Swing the heart's door open
freeing love and her company
sending them straight to the world
so that they plant there and grow
to bear all good things.

If faith slumbers too long,
or courage loses strength,
or desire grows dim—know
that nature's God is never far off
so call and answers will come.

Appeal to what is good and
endure for all noble pursuits.

Never lock the heart's door
though loss may come in,
for spring love will save you;
she will be a lamp for the heart.

Root yourself deep in trust and
grow in the sunlight of faith;
wrap your heart in the cloak of
courage to endure all dark moments.

Rest in God and
give birth to lofty dreams;
plant life's pillars in goodness
and know what is eternal
and what always fades.

Serve but the heart, for this a gift from God;
and whatever is of worth—cling to it.

Seek new shores though you may never land there,
and know that a little is a humble measure
of true happiness.

The Turning

Of that unknown height
that all our strivings inevitably
climb toward and reach,
there at the summit waits the Turning.

And from that overlook of events,
we may be fortunate and wise
to survey in reflection all that has passed our way thus far

To recall as much of what
the train of experience has shown us
while having conveyed us straight
to where we meet both our circumstance
and consequence—our Turning point.

And like Janus,
we ought to look both ways,
yet choosing only one:
either to go beyond or to stay.

And though to be still is wise wisdom is always a timely expense.

That no other time appears more real
to the mind than this—the
point of our Turning.

This time is a prevue for change;
that we either wed ourselves to courage
or we nurse our fears,
for the doors to either one will stand to face us squarely
at the end.

At our Turning point,
we must decide
to be brave or to cower,
to trust or to lose faith,
to move ahead or to retreat.

That destiny is our circumstance;
and that fate is our consequence.

The Way It Went

The leaves of love had long since fallen off;
it was not this that I misunderstood,
but it was the way that it all went.

Indeed, the season of love had changed.

Yet I did believe that love grows because of the light,
not ruins all that surrounds it like Holm's oak.

It went—this love affair,
evicted and sent from the heart;
for sure, my heart will be kissed no more by
love like this.

What more can be said?

But that the way it went still runs straight through me.

Treasure

The days go by so fast
as if they winged away,
never to come back.

Yet it was not time that vanished, but me.
And like a shadow marching towards dusk,
I did fade from your eyes.

I was hidden from love and
her company all the while.

Lost and far I did seem to be,
yet I knew no answer could satisfy your appeal.

But know that all the while you
were with me—there safe in memory as a
treasure to add to my happiness.

So remember, like all that is in the world,
you and I are forever one,
never are we apart, two in love, two in tempo—beating
so eternally.

Witness

Even in their full bloom the eyes missed you,

but once more your beauty streams across them
and faithfully they bloom.

The beautiful is the sun that makes all hearts bend.

For no beautiful thing is ever mislaid,
that each gets stored in that sacred under-story of imagination,
and there—below that divine canopy—
your captured beauty blooms eternally.

Words

Forever known we are by words though
we set them daily to rest in that invisible world.

Words immortalize us; they deify us.

With a stroke, a genius is made,
for many are so remembered.

Indeed, many have written their way into heaven.

And upon the soul's walls they have scribed divine
Scriptures; these coded secrecies that tell of what was and what
might be.

In these ink-spilled catacombs,
we find both altar and sanctuary:
we pay homage each time we resurrect
them from their shallow graves.

Holy is the power of the word, sacred and eternal.

Woven

Life churns—this way—that way—all about:
a rhythmic flow—through and throughout.

A long train of experience that passes in days,
an orchestrated span of time—this is life displayed.

Of our days, we weave them like needle and thread
sewing them into the tapestry
of soul and world.

Savor upon savor—life gets tasted in an inebriated degree of satisfaction,
yet daily fresh springs open
and there the old gives way to the new.

That need ignites the sparks of life—indeed,
and belief is the lamplight of all new discoveries.

Always, then, we ought to make imagination and soul the center,
for there we will find religion.

Epilogue

Know that all beginnings end.

From My Journal

Early morning note

Treasure the beautiful in all things.

F.M.J

Evening note

Make the mind a vista that soars above the clouds.

F.M.J.

Midnight note

Afterword

Pennames can serve us in two significant ways: they can offer us a sense of anonymity or a sense of identity. For me Ani Rumaer serves the latter. In a strange way, under another guise, we open doors that allow one or more of our Shadows to enter and take center stage. This is how it has been for me. The Shadow is both my inspiration and lamplight.

I hope, then, that you, too, have been inspired, especially to follow that narrow yet central path leading us towards the things we all truly desire— happiness. Though the road to happiness is paved with loss, sorrow and hardship that we remember, we can still have of its many pleasures and treasures. Like a rainbow, life is ever displayed in a myriad of colors; it is within the full spectrum of life itself that colorful experiences array us to help us build our Days, unfold our Dreams, and unlock the doors to our Shadows.

Happiness is within our capacity to have and enjoy in the course of a life time, so always endeavor to seek it with a courageous heart and with an open mind.

A.R.

Love, Faith and Destiny

Also available from PublishAmerica

TEENAGER RULES OR TEENAGERS RULE

by Tee Stuppiello

Teenager Rules or Teenagers Rule is a lighthearted, fun and real look at issues teens are dealing with today. It is filled with stories and "rules" acting as advice to help make it easier for pre-teens and teenagers to get through some of the most difficult times a girl may have to go through. Coming from the viewpoint of other teenagers, girls can easily relate to the stories and lessons that are meant to encourage self-esteem and make them aware of their own unique beauty, strength and the understanding they are not alone. With eight chapters in total, each created as a "handbook," they contain insightful, fun tales and "rules" to follow on being popular, being beautiful, getting away with lies, making a boy jealous, making a best friend, dealing with bullies and other teenage situations.

Paperback, 61 pages
6" x 9"
ISBN 1-60672-805-9

About the author:

Tee Stuppiello spent her childhood in central New Jersey where she resides with her daughters, Melody and Toni Lee, and fiancé, Bryan. The idea for *Teenager Rules or Teenagers Rule* came to her while spending time with her teenage daughter and her friends on a snowy winter day. She is in the process of writing *Teenagers Volume 2* and other stories.

Available to all bookstores nationwide.
www.publishamerica.com

THE HAND THAT SCARED JENNY

by Beverly Rosas

Whose hand did Jenny see reaching over the top of the backyard fence? Was it the wicked witch down the street? Was it the mysterious kidnapper? Jenny began an investigation, uncovering a shocking surprise.

Paperback, 46 pages
8.5" x 8.5"
ISBN 1-4241-9138-6

About the author:

Beverly Rosas is a special education teacher who works with children that have learning disabilities. Throughout her childhood, she approached every day as a new adventure. She sees that same sense of imagination in many of her students, and wants to encourage it in every child. This book is her way of inspiring that spark of imagination that is in us all.

SERENITY ISLE

by Adriana Vasquez

Serenity Isle is for the angry soul, the bitter heart that wonders for the answers in life. Healing is the question, the deepest sentiment within our heart waiting to explode from within. Emotions throughout life with love, with parents, with life as a whole that leaves scars in our heart. These poems comment meaningfully on life's sorrows, depressions and its hard moments…

The purpose is to help the reader see things the way life is, and despite all the problems we have in life it reassures the reader there is a light at the end of the tunnel.

Paperback, 132 pages
5.5" x 8.5"
ISBN 1-60610-509-4

About the author:

Adriana Vasquez Becerril was born in New York City. She currently works as a school principal in the Bronx, with a Ph.D. in school leadership from St. Johns University. Adriana has written other books like *Passages of Life*.

BARS, BEAM, FLOOR, VAULT, DEATH
by Diana Danali

Bars, Beam, Floor, Vault, Death is the story of a mother's need to bring to justice the gymnastics coach who abused her young daughters. Morgan Jensen, Kate Anderson, and Julie Murphy tolerate Tom Connor's cruelty for some time before realizing that he is practicing mind control on their innocent daughters. After finally rescuing their daughters from him, while risking their lives, they embark on a mission to discover who he really is and stop his evil ways. While on their journey of discovery they learn that he has changed his name and is a suspect in the murder of an eleven-year-old girl who trained at his former gymnastics facility. The three women encounter people from his past and gain the information they need to put an end to his abuse. They return to Colorado thinking they have enough evidence to confront the coach. However, Tom Connor proves to be more cunning than they had ever imagined.

Paperback, 160 pages
5.5" x 8.5"
ISBN 1-60610-467-5

About the author:

Diana Danali was born and raised in Canon City, Colorado, and has lived there most of her life. She was a gymnastics instructor for two years. For the past twelve years she has been a Curves multi-club owner and for two of those years she was also a mentor for Curves International, Inc. She opened the thirteenth Curves club in the world in Canon City in 1996. With the help of Curves International, Inc., she was instrumental in installing Curves circuits in the five women's correctional facilities in Colorado. She is currently working on her second manuscript.